A Sled Club

by Mara Padilla • illustrated by Bill Greenhead

"Look at the snow!

Can I sled?" Cliff yells.

Mom tells Cliff, "Yes."

"Cliff has a sled!

I want to go," Glen yells.

Dad tells Glen, "Yes, go."

What is this? Look at the red
flag. It is the Sled Club!

Cliff gets on his sled.

Glen slips. Glen plops.

Kids plod up the hill.

Kids flip. Kids flop.

Kids sled down the hill.

Sleds slip. Sleds slide.

Cliff claps. Glen claps.

The kids slap. Go, Sled Club!